Rookie Read-About® Science

Sound All Around

By Fay Robinson

Consultants:
Robert L. Hillerich, Professor Emeritus,
Bowling Green State University, Bowling Green, Ohio
Consultant, Pinellas County Schools, Florida

Lynne Kepler, Educational Consultant

CHILDRENS PRESS®
CHICAGO

Design by Lindaanne Donohoe

Library of Congress Cataloging-in-Publication Data

Robinson, Fay.
    Sound all around/by Fay Robinson.
        p.   cm. — (Rookie read-about science)
    ISBN 0-516-06024-4
    1. Sound — Juvenile literature. 2. Sounds — Juvenile literature.
[1. Sound.]   I. Title. II. Series: Robinson, Fay. Rookie read-about science.

QC225.5.R62 1994
534 — dc20   93-3859
                                                                          CIP
                                                                          AC

What sounds can you make?

Can you
snap your fingers . . .

play a drum . . .

moo like a cow?

Almost everything you do
makes a sound.

Listen closely as you turn
this page.

But what exactly is sound?

To understand,
pluck a rubber band.

Do you see how the rubber
band moves back and forth
very quickly? Do you hear
the sound it makes?

For there to be sound,
something must move

back and forth, or vibrate.

Put your hand on your
throat and sing.

Do you feel your throat
vibrate?

Put the palm of one hand
on the door and knock
with the other hand.

Do you feel the door
vibrate?

Musical instruments
all have parts that vibrate.

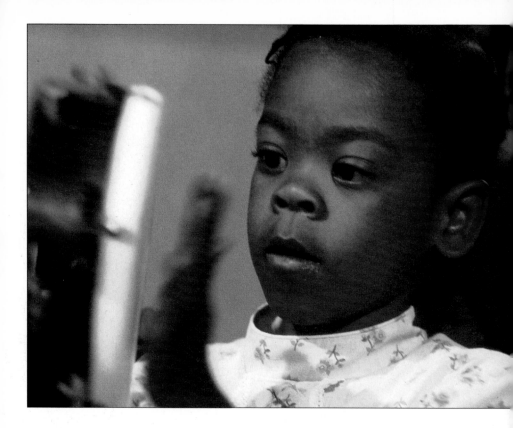

How does sound get from
a rubber band, a door, or
a musical instrument to
your ears?

Sound travels through the air
in waves — sound waves.

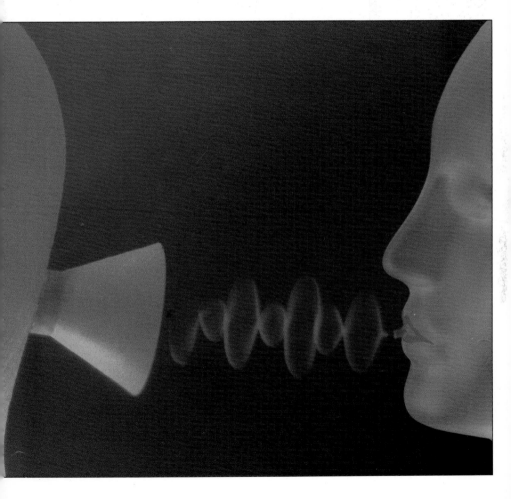

Sound waves are invisible.

If you could see them, they might look a little like the waves a pebble makes as it plunks into a pond.

Sound waves move out from an object in all directions.

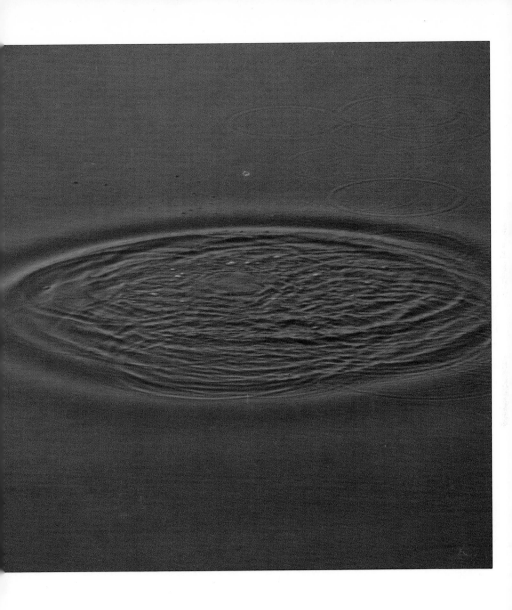

They reach your ears very quickly, and you hear the sound.

Sound travels through water
more easily than air.

This is why you hear bubbles and splashes so well under water.

Some whales sing songs
that can be heard for miles
in the ocean.

Sound travels even better through solids.

Put your ear to the floor and listen as a friend walks away.

Sounds are all different.

Trains make very loud
sounds.

Raindrops make very soft
sounds.

The loudness or softness
of a sound is called its volume.

A squeaky gate makes a high sound.

A mooing cow makes a
low sound.

The highness or lowness
of a sound is called its pitch.

Sounds are important.
Some sounds warn you to
move out of the way.

Some sounds tell you
someone is at the door.

Some sounds are voices,
calling you to come out
and play.

Even when you're alone
in the quiet of your bed,
there are sounds all around.

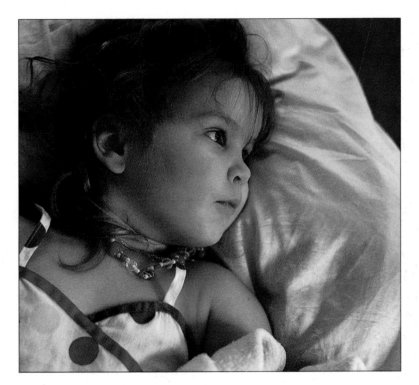

Listen. Do you hear them?

Words You Know

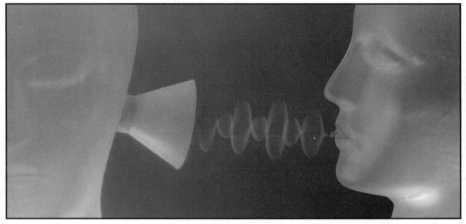

sound waves

vibrate

musical instruments

rubber band

30

volume

train (loud sound)

raindrops (soft sound)

pitch

ueaky gate (high sound)

mooing cow (low sound)

Index

About the Author

Fay Robinson is an early childhood specialist who lives and works in the Chicago area. She received a bachelor's degree in Child Study from Tufts University and a master's degree in Education from Northwestern University. She has taught preschool and elementary children and is the author of several picture books.

Photo Credits

PhotoEdit – ©David Young-Wolff, Cover, 5, 22, 31 (top left); ©Robert Brenner, 7; ©Tony Freeman, 8, 15, 18, 30, (bottom right); ©Merritt A. Vincent, 11; ©Alan Oddie, 12; ©Richard Hutchings, 16; ©John Neubauer, 24, 31 (bottom left); ©Tom MCarthy, 30 (bottom left)

Photri – ©MacDonald Photography, 29

SuperStock International, Inc. – 13, 30 (top); ©D. Spindel, 9; ©T. Nakamura, 19

Valan – ©J. Eastcott/Y. Momatiuk, 3; ©Tom W. Parkin, 6; ©Paul Janosi, 17; ©Richard Nowitz, 21; ©Harold V. Green, 23, 31 (top right); ©Ken Patterson, 25, 31 (bottom right); ©Gilles Delisle, 26; ©Jean Bruneau, 27; ©Kennon Cooke, 28

COVER: Girl making sounds